BOA

EDITIONS LTD

Transitory

Transitory

Subhaga Crystal Bacon

AMERICAN POETS CONTINUUM SERIES, NO. 204

BOA EDITIONS, LTD. ⌛ ROCHESTER, NY ⌛ 2023

First Edition
23 24 25 26 7 6 5 4 3 2 1

For information about permission to reuse any material from this book, please contact The Permissions Company at www.permissionscompany.com or e-mail permdude@gmail.com.

Publications by BOA Editions, Ltd.—a not-for-profit corporation under section 501 (c) (3) of the United States Internal Revenue Code—are made possible with funds from a variety of sources, including public funds from the Literature Program of the National Endowment for the Arts; the New York State Council on the Arts, a state agency; and the County of Monroe, NY. Private funding sources include the Max and Marian Farash Charitable Foundation; the Mary S. Mulligan Charitable Trust; the Rochester Area Community Foundation; the Ames-Amzalak Memorial Trust in memory of Henry Ames, Semon Amzalak, and Dan Amzalak; the LGBT Fund of Greater Rochester; and contributions from many individuals nationwide. See Colophon on page 94 for special individual acknowledgments.

Cover Art: Flying Nests by Sugandhi Katharine Barnes
Cover Design: Sandy Knight
Interior Design and Composition: Isabella Madeira
BOA Logo: Mirko

BOA Editions books are available electronically through BookShare, an online distributor offering Large-Print, Braille, Multimedia Audio Book, and Dyslexic formats, as well as through e-readers that feature text to speech capabilities.

Cataloging-in-Publication Data is available from the Library of Congress.

BOA Editions, Ltd.
250 North Goodman Street, Suite 306
Rochester, NY 14607
www.boaeditions.org
A. Poulin, Jr., Founder (1938-1996)

For All the Trans and Gender Non-Conforming Lights Extinguished in 2020

'*[P]oetry of witness*' . . . *doesn't mean to write about political matters; it means to write out of having been . . . incised or even wounded by something that happened in the world.*

Carolyn Forché,
Prismatics: Larry Levis and Contemporary American Poetry

Contents

Cautiously Watching for Violence

August 2020: the month of no murders of trans people

His voice at the end of the line, middle of the night,
bored and languorous, described what he
would do to me, knowing where I lived.
> *I'm going to come where you live*
> *and rape you and kill you*
as if he was following a script. The telephone—
1981, a plastic-shelled landline—waking me. The bed
against the wall, between windows overlooking the street
in my hometown, the town where I lived the first 20 years
of my life, so known—me to it, and it to me. I was tired
of the threats.
> Men calling me to tell me these things.
> Men speaking about me in loud voices from the bar
> while I bought a six pack of beer, saying who I was
> and what.
> Men intentionally banging into me, their bodies
> like bars surrounding me, hands in my hair, breath
> in my face.
Years and years by telephone, on streets, when I was lean
and rangy in torn jeans and sheer shirts, biker boots,
even once by an old Russian woman in Brooklyn,
and later by a car full of men following. Even then,
I shouted them down, shouted them off, walking
in the daylight somewhere in New York City,
always the angry mouth that talked back.

A psychic once said that I have the unique aura
of those who in their lifetimes migrate from male
to female. I knew this was true, having known
myself a boy and then riding that knowing into puberty,
confused in skirts and fishnets and desert boots.
Crushes on girls.

With cheekbones like knives.
Who pushed into my lavatory stall.
Who let me wear her leather jacket.
Who was pregnant and married at 17.
Whose hair I stroked by flashlight.
Who embarrassed my dreams with longing.

The pressure for dance dates,
the gay boy smelling of beer,
the boy who never called,
the one who was refused,
the son of a butcher,
the cousin of a friend,
the friend of my brother.

I lost my virginity when I was nineteen, in college,
to a man twelve years my senior I thought I'd marry,
who wore women's perfume, did manual labor,
owned a dress shop with his mother, and dumped
me for a younger woman pregnant with his child.

Years and years, women and men, the flush
of yin and yang in me.
Big hair, red lips, short skirts,
colored tights and shoes and boots
and leather jackets in many colors.
The wide legged stride said
don't fuck with me
an irresistible invitation to do just that.

Even, at sixty, walking my foofy dog across the street
in the suburbs, a spring day, from the car window
he says *get out of the way you ugly old dyke.*
Dyke. Cunt. Bitch. Even, once, Faggot.

Listen: there's a way that I'm as queer and trans
as you can be despite my *femininity*: hair to my waist,
eyeliner, and inside, the man I've always known myself to be.
It's a kind of drag, the girl over the boy within the girl.
Tight jeans, big belt, even under my elderly paunch, still
that fire that says let me scorch you/scorch me with desire.

Justice: An Acrostic

(A Catalog of Trans Murders in the First Half of 2020)

Just driving a taxi in Oklahoma was deadly for Dustin Parker, 25.
Using the women's bathroom killed Alexa, homeless in Puerto Rico—
social media led her killers to her. Yampi Mendez Arocho's profile—*Fuck love*—
tells his story; dead at 19. Monika Diamond, honored LGBTQ mothers through the
International Mother of the Year Pageant: misgendered, deadnamed, 34, North Carolina.
Caught with a stolen wig, in Harlem, Lexi, "Ebony" Sutton, 33, loved poetry and
everyone she met. Johanna Metzger, 25, self-taught musician who could play

just about any instrument, stabbed in Maryland. Serena Angelique Vasquez, 31,
using vacation time to visit her friend Layla Pelaez Sánchez, 21, in Puerto Rico, both
shot, their bodies burned. Then Penélope Díaz Ramírez, in the Baymon Correctional Center,
time done in a men's prison. Nina Pop, in Missouri, 28, stabbed in her apartment.
I love myself now . . . looking at the pictures before I transitioned, Helle Jae O'Regan, 20,
cleaning the barbershop in Texas where she worked; stabbed. Tallahassee police accosted him
even though he had no weapons, said *Stop moving, n----r,* ending Tony McDade.

June 9, Rem'mie Fells, pulled from the Schuykill, legless; *she lived her truth so loud*
u could hear her a mile away. An 18-year-old boy and 14-year-old girl led by an adult man
shot Riah Milton, home health worker, 25, in Ohio. Jayne Thompson, shot by police,
troubled in her transition in Colorado. Bail was refused for an 18-year-old student
in Chicago, who went home with Selena Reyes-Hernandez, and learning she was trans
came back later *mad as hell*, and shot her nine times. Brayla Stone, 17, Arkansas,
evidence of hate crime absent, was left in a car by another teen charged with a prior death.

Just an hour ago, arrested while I'm writing, the man who killed Merci Mack, 22, Dallas,
unless she release a video of them together, shot her multiple times. One of five found dead
since the start of July: Shaki Peters, 32, Amite, Louisiana; Bree Black, 27, July 3, shot
too. Summer Taylor, white, non-binary killed after a car drove into a crowd of protestors
in Seattle, Washington, on July 4 at the Black Femme March, not yet ruled a homicide, be-
cause driving a car into a group of protestors, on Independence Day, is apparently
excusable or—what? Manslaughter?—binary loophole that says: not woman, not murder.

Dustin Parker, 25, McAlester, OK, January 1

Cold in McAlester, Oklahoma, in January.
For those not fit to drive, New Year's Day,
Dustin drove his Rover Cab to help them home
for free.
      I saw him at 6:15, 6:20, and he
was pronounced dead at 6:30. That still shakes me.
Why didn't I hug him?
                   his wife, Regina, said.

The first day of the year, first transgender
murder of the year, Dustin Parker,
husband, father of four, shot point blank

through the window of his cab. His face
in the obituary photo, young and sweet,
open as the first day of the year.

Alexa: Neulisa Luciano Ruiz, 28, Tao Baja, Puerto Rico, February 24

They didn't kill a man in a skirt. They killed Alexa.

Because it is allowed, they taunted her always
and everywhere. In the photograph that went viral
online in Puerto Rico,

                    after she was falsely accused
                    of spying on a woman
                    in the bathroom of McDonalds,

she looks like a nun, the white towel on her head
like a wimple, her black coat.
                          But there's her purse,
the mirror that was her safety to see who might be
behind her.
            The photo allowed them to track her down
and kill her in a park in *Toa Baja*.

       Hey, can you give me some of that ass,
       We are going to shoot you up.
       Let's spin the tires on this motherfucker.
       You bet I am going to go and shoot him.

In the headlights' glare, ten shots, laughter
on the video they shared on social media
because it is allowed.

Yampi Mendez Arocho, 19, Moca, Puerto Rico, March 5

Fuck love; I don't believe in it anymore.

The day before you were killed, Yampi, this is what you wrote.
Now I'm left wondering, is that what the world gave you?

There's not enough to answer the questions:

>   The woman who assaulted you five hours before?
>   Did you go home for help from your mother,
>   who reported the assault to the police?

Then you were dead.

>   This we know: shot twice in the face and twice in the back
>   in the community playground, in Moca, where you grew up.

The day before you were shot, a selfie in front of a mirror—

>   There's a blue-eyed tiger tattooed on the back of your left hand,
>   a cross on your right forearm. Your shoulders are wide
>   under a turquoise shirt, diagonal lines of red flamingos

>   all rest on one leg. The nails on your slender fingers
>   are long. A thin rectangular pendant hangs on silver chain
>   down your chest. Your face is narrow, fox like.

Deeply set shadowed eyes look at your phone.
Flamingos represent an open heart, balance, grace.
Yampi, where is your gaze?

John Scott/Scottlyn Kelly DeVore, 51, Augusta, GA, March 12

He still had the same heart no matter what he looked like, which was a good heart, a kind heart.

Authorities found the body of a missing man thought to have been murdered.
Wearing a white dress and a blond wig, on March 12 he left home
without returning.

Someone called the police when he was missing two days further.
He went out dressed as Scottlyn. After two weeks dead and alone,
what authorities found was the body of a man who'd been murdered.

For Scott's loved ones, a nightmare that's unending. Waiting for the confirming words,
while cleaning out his house—two weeks without news cuts to the bone:
the fear that someone killed the friend who's not returning.

The killer who waited outside the apartment must have felt some ardor
for that *Beautiful angel heart, best friend, idol,* and in the dark, unknown,
left the body thought to be a man who'd been murdered.

After strangling her, he put her body in the trunk of her car to transport her,
toss in a dumpster in that last bit of spring air, then went back to take all she owned,
knowing she was not returning.

Nearly midnight, so little light, the waning moon in its last quarter,
he was there, waiting to kill her. How can he atone
for the body of this gender-fluid man he murdered?
Neither Scott nor Scottlyn will be returning.

Monika Diamond, 34, Charlotte, NC, March 18

Monika, *chosen mother to all,*
despite your dress and beautiful smile,
they misgendered and deadnamed you,
█████████████, at your death
in the parking lot of the Days Inn.

> The police reported *a man*
> said *he* was having trouble
> breathing, in the ambulance
> being treated, that *man* (you Monika),
> asked for *his friend* to come
> into the ambulance with *him.*

Refused entry, your friend, Monika,
came back with a gun and shot you
several times, multiple times,
killing you, Monika.

It's the sixth anniversary
of the International Mother
of the Year Pageant. You said,

> *I want to give something back*
> *to the mothers in the LGBT community*
> *to say thanks for what you do as a mother*
> *in the LGBT community and this pageant*
> *is for the female in the LGBT community*
> *that is a Drag, FIEF or Transgender.*

Your own people, Monika; your own words,
your own name, Monika Diamond: beauty
pressed from rock.

Lexi, "Ebony" Sutton, 33, Harlem, NY, March 28

Lexi of the House of Ebony.

There's a scarcity of details once again
despite there being witnesses at the scene:
they say you stole somebody's wig that night.

Were you working, waiting, resting, Lexi,
on that park bench where you were last seen?
There's a scarcity of details once again.

At 1:30 in the morning, Lexi, what brought
the man on the red scooter racing?
They say it was the wig you stole that night.

They say the man on the scooter stabbed you twice
in the neck, then fled into the dark on that red machine.
There's a scarcity of details once again:

some didn't see a scooter red or white.
They say they overheard you being
blamed for stealing a wig that night.

You're the fifth one killed so far this year,
Lexi. I wish I knew more about your life.
There must be more than wig and scooter here;
there's a scarcity of details once again.
You can't have died for a stolen wig that night.

Transition/Transmission

for Matthew/Crystyl

Crystyl, Crystyl my drag sister
with an extra *y* in my old name
the broken *x* that makes us *them*,
all big hair and war paint, sequins
and furs. Video transforms him.
A hand waved over the lens—
presto change-o reveals him Divine.

His cookie-baking, fish-catching, son-loving self
transmuted to High Femme, the light in his eyes
the same.

Johanna Metzger, 25, Baltimore, MD, April 11

Jo was not attacked because of who she was; she was not the target, wrong time, wrong place.

I'm sorry, Christine. I stalked your Facebook page to learn
about Johanna Metzger, the trans woman stabbed on the street
while in rehab at Safe Haven in Baltimore, identified as your child.

You say that Johanna was not killed for who she was.

For you, Johanna never existed, only your *son,* ▉. It's *his* image
on your profile, and funeral pictures where *he,* your *son,* ▉
his hair cut short, wears a black suit in *his* coffin. You say
you'll bury *his* ashes with you; want to name a star for *him.*

You say that Johanna was not killed for who she was.

On her Facebook page where she had *No friends to show,*
she identified herself as Johanna
      in fingerless black gloves,
      an off the shoulder shirt over camisole,
      her blonde hair long,
      her smoky eye makeup,
      and, with glasses or without,
      her steady gaze.
Of her love interests, she said: *It's complicated since September 2019.*

After her death, you wrote: if u could only go back 3 years my son would be alive.

No ashes to bury. Her star's a pentangle, the last picture posted two months before she died.
What haven did she seek in Baltimore in April, becoming her place and time?

Maybe it's time to untangle, Christine, her identity from your own.

Penélope Díaz Ramírez, 31, Bayamon, Puerto Rico, April 13

The third in eight days.

April 13, *lost to violence*
which, it turns out means
beaten and hanged to death
at the Bayamon correctional complex,
a men's prison in Puerto Rico.

A men's prison, Penélope.

Why did it take two weeks
to announce your death?

I have more questions than answers
Penélope, not even an image of you
survives to those like me, an outsider
like you.

       Penélope: weaver, faithful,
long suffering, wise and wily,
your name is strong. Did you weave
and unravel your own shroud
as the days passed to stave off crude
suitors? My mind stops at your end.

Serena Angelique Vasquez, 31 & Layla Pelaez Sánchez, 21, Humacao, Puerto Rico, April 21: An Erasure

Extracts from the FBI affidavit reported in the Washington Blade, May 4, 2020

Two men   murder   two transgender women

                                        Sean Díaz   19, "wanted to shoot and
kill" Layla Pelaez   they "had sexual relations"

                        Juan Carlos Pagán   21, and Serena Angelique Velázquez
        "had sexual relations"   Díaz   told Pagan
that Velázquez was Trans.

  Díaz   wanted to   kill both
                        for tricking them

                                Pelaez
proposed   marihuana to   talk a little more.

                        Pelaez gave Pagán the keys   Díaz
        "shot and killed" the two Trans women while   driving
                                                        under a bridge

                                                                        set the
vehicle on fire   the   bodies inside

Nina Pop, 28, Sikeston, MO, May 3

We marked safe; we on the safe board.

Saturday, May 2, the day before you were stabbed multiple times
at home, you wrote:
> *nt nothing like getting up jamming and deep
> cleaning yo house on a Saturday morning! My house is spotless anyway
> but ant nothing like a Saturday morning deep clean that's a whole vibe.*

Last days of *stay home*, you were ready to get out, clean house or no.

Sunday night, your joy spilled onto New Madrid Street, phone video on,
eyelashes, and that cropped *Baddest Babe* hoodie.
Watching your face,
hearing your voice for 15 minutes 32 seconds, just hanging out, looking for your cousin,
Ellery, you come through clearly,
Missouri drawl, the way you drank
from that tall Styrofoam cup and straw, your face lit by car lights.

You said *I'm not going in that open space.* Keeping safe in the celebration.

What happened next, only you and he know,
and neither of you is speaking.

It took 3 weeks, but know that they got him, Nina.

He pled not guilty, despite the crime scene being against him.

It's not much solace, I guess, but they had help;
many called to give information.
It was a hate crime, Nina, no doubt in their minds.

Helle Jae O'Regan, 20, San Antonio, TX, May 6

I love myself now. Thank you to everyone who's ever supported me and to anyone who hasn't
I hope you come around.

Damion Campbell came around, but not to love her.

The barbershop closed for quarantine since March,
she and the crew inside were cleaning when he tried
the lock. They let him in. May 6, two days
before reopening, three past her birthday.

He asked for an appointment, gave his real name
and phone number. Went out to get his backpack
in order to pay, and came back with a gun and knife.
He said,

> *God sent me to kill you for doing something wrong.*
> *What have you done wrong? What have you done wrong?*
> *God sent me here to kill you because you have done something wrong!*
> *What have you done wrong?*

He didn't want money, or the computer. He put
Helle in a choke hold and when she lost consciousness,
stabbed her prone body multiple times.

He killed Helle as God's instrument of death
though there's *nothing to indicate hate.*

Jayne Thompson, 33, Mesa County, CO, May 9, 2020: Misgendered for a Month

"Since she came out, life was very different," Leopardi said. "Everything changed. A lot of things started weighing on her mentally."

Being a cisgender male, she said, was easy,
then, transitioning, people didn't trust her as much.
Her children's mother didn't accept her change.
At the bar in Bisbee, Arizona, tourists were rude,
men would bump into her hoping for a fight.

No one knows what she was doing in Orchard Mesa
that day. Clearly, she was lost. Standing by the road
for over an hour with a stick across her arms
like a mannequin. She just stood there, doing nothing
illegal. But someone called 911 anyway. Worried, maybe.

Clearly, she was troubled. To the officer's questions,
she was unresponsive, then aggressive, wielding a knife.

The cop who shot her took her for a man with a shaggy beard.
He said she lunged with the knife, so he shot her.
Multiple times, it turns out, even after she was down.
It was a month before they corrected her gender and name.

Jayne.

Her co-worker Liz said she doesn't even know
where she's buried. She said:

> *Every night when I would*
> *drop her off at home, she would say,*
> *'Goodnight, I love you, Liz.'*
> *That would be the last thing*
> *we would say to each other.*

Tony McDade, 38, Tallahassee, FL, May 27

Somebody that I gave my loyalty to allowed her son and nephews to jump me.

Let's be clear. You wanted to kill those
who jumped you, five against one,
beat you in a fetal position.

> You wanted to kill, even, yourself—
> made many attempts—or in a shootout
> with the cops, who, you said: *they see a gun*
> *they just shoot . . . So that's what I'm pushing for,*
> *because I don't want to be here*
> *on earth dealing with the government.*

Some say, Tony, that the government isn't responsible
        for our lives or your death.
They're not responsible
        for our health and safety, for our liberty, and justice.
Some say, Tony, that you were a girl, some a man.

After you stabbed Malik with a knife, payback for the fight,
the cops hunted you to the Leon Arms, and there, at 10:59 am,
someone said,

> *I just heard pow pow pow pow pow,*
> *so I'm like damn they shooting early in the day time,*
> *it's day time they shooting.*

Tony, they say you pulled a gun, pointed a gun,
so shots were fired, and then you were gone.

Selena Reyes-Hernandez, 37, Chicago, IL, May 31

He kept seeing her face, so he went back there to do it again.

Selena, everything about this is wrong, murdered for being trans
by an 18-year-old—it's hard to say man—high school student
who lived two blocks away from you and owned the Luger
he killed you with after coming home with you for sex.

At 18, every boy becomes a man, even if he's still in high school—
old enough to vote, to own a gun, to pick up a woman at 5 am—
to get in her car and then go home with her intending to have sex.
Selena, you can't have known he'd react this way to who you were.

Being old enough to vote, to own a gun, to pick up a woman at 5 am—
why would you expect that he would kill you because you were trans?
Selena, you can't have known he'd react this way to who you were,
that he'd go home to get a gun to shoot you, then shoot you again.

You certainly never expected that he would kill you for being trans.
You brought him home, you washed his hands, then he asked, and you said.
So he went home for the gun and came back to shoot you again, then again,
to kill you Selena because who you were, he said, made him mad.

Of Band Fags and Hate Mail

In the eighties when I taught high school in the burgers-
and-beer suburbs of the New Jersey Pine Barrens,
Air Force brats and professors' kids interbred
a miasma of shame and fear. I was newly thirty
and confused about how to dress, walk in heels,
and wear my hair, how not to appear too queer.

I taught freshman English, coached 3 sports (and dance),
advised the literary magazine. So many late days
bled into the flagrant dusk to wait outside with the freshly
showered, hooded bodies. If they were slow to emerge
from the locker room, the threat was always the same:
you'll have to ride the last bus with the band fags.

Mornings, I'd arrive before homeroom with the kids
who had jobs and worked half days. The boys would hide
in the lav, halls empty, echoing with shouts of *DYKE*
while I clicked my way to the staff room. I'd like to say
they were better, my peers, who spread rumors that I
was dating the *gay girl* athlete who'd attached herself to me.

When I escaped high school for community college, hate
was delivered to my mailbox after hours: *Crystal Bacon,
you worthless piece of shit. You're so ugly you can't get a man
so you do unnatural things with women.* I read it out loud
in class to look for the guilty: young woman, back row,
failing Comp, who slid out early and never returned.

Ask me, I might write from out here on the left coast
in the youth of the twenty-first century, *what difference
their strongest love or hate has made.* I'll tell you:
freedom from fear; wholeness is what they gave.

Dominique "Rem'mie" Fells, Philadelphia, PA, June 8

To be successful, take care of my mother, and have an impact.

These were her three wishes as told to the man
with the video camera that day on the street
in Kensington. Also: *just know the next time*
you all see me I'm going to be somebody
not just on YouTube, on television.

She took the sidewalk with a sashay, showing off
in short shorts and shearling boots those long legs.

Rem'mie was just always having a good time
and laughing. We have a lot of family get-togethers,
she loved being around her cousins, uncles and aunts.
She likes to eat and have a good time.

Her mother said: *Tolerance and acceptance*
should be a natural, common way of life.

The evening of June 8, Rem'mie's body
was pulled from the Schuylkill River
with trauma to the head and face, stab wounds—
which by some kind of grace—is what killed her
before both legs were severed at the thigh.

      Who does that?

They're looking for the man, an acquaintance,
in whose home they found *a cutting tool*, and blood.

There were 27 trans women killed last year.
Halfway through this one it's nearly the same.

At her funeral, which spilled out into the street,
the minister said: *We're fighting against racism,
classism, homophobia . . . Hate running rampant.
Black lives matter. LGBT Black lives matter too.*

Her sister said: *I have never felt more pain
than choosing the casket
that's my sister's final resting place.
Every day I wake up and I see her face.*

Riah Milton, 25, Liberty Twp, OH, June 9

Ohio does not have a hate crime statute that includes sexual orientation or gender identity.

Riah, your picture captivated me. Full-figured,
long lashed, shapely brows, and bow mouth,
your soft face framed by hair in twists worn long
down your back, a beautiful woman.

They say that two teenagers used the Internet
to *lure* you to a park to steal your car. What
did they promise? When you got there, you
understood. The boy, 18, shot you and accidentally
himself. The girl is fourteen, the juvenile lover
of a 25-year-old man they're still seeking.

On the map, Liberty Township is a swanky swath
of lawns, and parks dotted with McMansions,
and creeks thick with trees. They sought you, Riah,
you who *just wanted to be accepted,* and lured you
to that place of green to kill you and steal your car.

Asked if you were targeted because you were trans
the Ohio police said:

> *This person was lured there*
> *to be robbed and to have his car . . .*
> *his belongings taken.*

Brian "Egypt" Powers, 43, Akron, OH, June 13: An Acrostic

He knew so many people . . . He never met a stranger in his life.

Transgender is a blanket word for all who fall outside the
Realm of gender types. It's not an indication that someone is
A person who's changed their gender assignment or
Now uses *they* pronouns. No. One assigned male at birth
Still can use *he* pronouns and live a unique expression of
Gender beyond Gay. Brian was such a one. 6'4, sometimes
Eyebrows arched, and hair in *unicorn* braids of varied colors,
Now and then curls, or shaved short, and generally
Dressed for comfort. Brian who was also known in Akron as
Egypt. Staunch supporter of the LGBTQ+ community,
Recovering, and living stably, working as a cook, which he loved.

Paula Abdul back-up dancer was his childhood dream.
Even though it never came to pass, he still reminisced about it.
Racism, transphobia, or random violence, it's still unclear who
Shot Egypt through the thighs and left him to die
On a bit of grass off the University of Ohio campus.
Nobody's come forward to help solve the crime.*

Brayla Stone, 17, Little Rock, AK, June 25

You gotta forgive me if u feel I'm too much.

Brayla, there *was* a lot of you to reckon with for only 17.
Your Facebook page is full of photos of you in pinup
pose, your tongue stuck out, these interspersed
frequently with the faith that *God got my back.*
The paradox gives me whiplash. I feel very old
and very white swimming up from your social media sites.

The wigs of many colors, the clothes likewise,
and eyelashes the size of butterfly wings. I feel
your fight, your will to not just live but to thrive.

Seventeen in Little Rock, Arkansas, and someone
paid five thousand dollars to have you killed
by another teenager who already once beat
a murder charge.   Your body was left in a car
on a walking path in a suburb called Sherwood,
which is ironic in a sad way, with its innocent
suggestions of Robin Hood and Maid Marian.
There's no indication of a hate crime, Arkansas
being one of four states in which they don't exist.

Forgive us, Brayla, for not being enough for you.

Merci Mack Richey, 22, Dallas, TX, June 30

I really feel for the victim's family because this now puts them through further grief.

Merci, their case fell apart. Someone said they saw you
being chased and shot by ██████████ who bullied you
in middle school. Only you two know what happened
in the days before your death, the video you planned
to release.

        Some said it started in your teens, his teasing,
taunting, then as adults—
           you videotaped *getting nasty* with him,
threatened to post it on Snapchat. Then you fought.

A witness saw someone they thought was him shoot you
while you ran through the parking lot, then stand
over your fallen, your small body, and shoot
you again.
        Merci, the stories got changed, statements revoked.
        For you, two years out, no justice, no mercy.

Shaki Peters, 32, Amite City, LA, July 1

She was full of laughter and an abundance of life.

Shaki, there's a plant that grows here, where I live,
called Shadbush—it's also known as Service Berry—
but it's the genus I thought of yesterday, seeking shade
on the hillside, carrying you with me in the heat of day.
How it gives shade, gives fruit, dark purple, seeded,
and nourishing.
                    Your face, Shaki, in the one photo
I can find, is round and open, dark and sweet. Your eyes
seem to tip up a bit at the outer corners. Your lips
are full, plush as pillows. I keep waiting for some story
to explain your murder. I don't know how much
that matters in the long run, but it might fill the gap
around your death.
                        I keep thinking about the name Amite
City from the French for friendship. Like my hometown,
Philadelphia, City of Brotherly Love. Likewise,
no friend to trans women.
                            I spent a month in Louisiana
in 1984. It was hot and humid and I loved the way sweat
soaked me, sticking clothes to skin. I used to move
from shade to shade, the shadows of buildings,
banana trees, and one very large fig tree in the yard
of the house I rented, hand-shaped leaves the size of fans.

In 1984, Shaki, you weren't even born yet. It was a heyday
for being Queer if you don't count AIDS. We were all
trying on gender like a wig or a dress or suit and tie.
I used to go to a drag bar in Philly where I had a crush
on a zaftig redhead I now know to have been trans.
She was very kind to me, taking my face in her soft hands,
fragrant and styled like the mother of a childhood friend
I had to share a bed with one weekend. I clung all night
to the far edge in fear that I would accidentally touch her.
There was a ripeness in her, sweet, nourishing, a kind
of femme that makes my heart ache, that I've never known
or been. There are many kinds of shadow, Shaki, many kinds
of shade. I think of you now inhabiting that: luscious, lush, safe.

Bree Black, 27, Pompano Beach, FL, July 3

The average life expectancy of a Black trans woman is 35 years of age.

Like everyone, what she wanted from life was independence,
just the usual American dream with its varied and fixed rewards:
health, the safety to travel, to walk without fear on the street,
and at the end of the day, when it was time to sleep, silence.
She wanted to live and be recognized in the world as a woman,
who could keep a job, enjoy her life, and have her own crowd.

That weekend, on her own block, close to home, in the crowd
was someone who shot her and ended her hard-won independence.
No one can say if she was shot because she was a trans woman.
The Sheriff's department increased its initial offer of a reward
in hopes that someone will want the money enough to break silence
about what they saw, and who killed Bree by gunshot in the street.

Even after ten o'clock, it's brazen to shoot someone in the street
in the midst of a large and rowdy holiday weekend crowd.
Someone must have heard the shot even if it was far from silent
being a loud holiday, fireworks, and music to celebrate Independence
Day. But keeping silent about witnessing a killing has its rewards
regardless of who did the shooting, and that the victim was a trans woman.

American Independence didn't change life for American women,
or most men. Black people were expected to step into the street
if they met a white person. If they didn't, they reaped a violent reward,
public humiliation at least, or flogging before an angry crowd.
No. It was a long time before many got what you could call independence,
the freedom to learn, work, vote, marry who they loved, and break silence

about the many and unsubtle ways this country continued to try to silence them. Jim Crow, and the marriage laws that essentially treated all women as property. *Don't forget the ladies!* So much for American independence. Still, many feel patriotism or at least the desire to celebrate in the streets, gather together to barbecue, parade, drink beer and, in Florida, crowd the beaches. Then, once it's dark, a fireworks display is their just reward.

Bree went out, close to home, to be part of the action, to celebrate, and her reward— American, taxpayer, employee, her parents' child—was to be forever silenced there, shot by an unseen killer who disappeared into the holiday crowd. Twenty-seven years old, she was the tenth Black and nineteenth trans woman killed in the first seven months of the year. Shot and left dead in the street. You have to wonder what there is to celebrate when there's so little independence.

Summary Taylor, 24, Seattle, WA, July 4

They were always the first one to call people out for being sexist, racist — standing up for queer and trans people . . . they were the one that was so vocal.

Dancing the Cupid Shuffle wearing a Black
Lives Matter t-shirt, protective gloves,
a mask around their chin, Summer Taylor,
activist, sibling, child, animal lover,
killed by a car driven the wrong way
up a closed ramp into the crowd.

Summer, white, non-binary, Seattleite
had all the privilege of race, love, family
support, college, meaningful work, and strength
of conviction fed on these nutrients.

They stopped to dance on their way to City Hall
at 5:30 in the morning, another nightlong
protest, the Black Femme March, festive,
a celebration, the Interstate closed, a space
created for them to stand together.

The day before, Diaz Love, injured
in the crash, posted on Facebook: *the death threats
from hate groups is real, real this weekend.*
Love, recovering, in pain, the threats keep
coming, writes: *If they thought this murder
would make us back down, they are wrong.*

Summer, the last death in the first half
of 2020, stands in stark relief
for what they stood for: Black trans
femme sisters, trans brothers, femme
dykes and gay boys, white, black, brown
the rainbow of gender no car can mow down.

Why I'm Writing About the Murders of Trans & Gender Nonconforming People in the Year of COVID

Once I started, I couldn't stop. Every day,
I lifted the bandage to see the latest wound,
infection spreading to rot.

I was asked to write a poem about social justice,
Black Lives Matter, gun violence. A Queer
person who's survived to elderhood,

I wrote about this intersection of fears
an epidemic beyond even the epidemic of the year.
Suspended in time—sunlit window,

feet on the red rug of my room, a new day,
Googling trans murders—I was whole before,
and a hole after. So fast in July: Marilyn,

Dior, Queasha, Aja, then the long break,
two-week vacation. I kept my vigil
even prayed daily: *let it be over. Please,*

no more. Then came Kee, August thirteenth,
and two weeks later, Lea, the end of the month,
and Elie Che, drowned off Jones Beach, maybe

an accident, like Isabella after Labor Day,
who fell or was pushed from a roof.
No proof in either case of a crime. Fall

brought the death of Aerrion Burnett, shot
in Independence; Mia, by her boyfriend
in Philadelphia. Michellyn, the sixth to die

in Puerto Rico, but not the last. By October
it was clear that the year would surpass
the one before and the one before that. Brook

the thirty-second, twenty years old, the twenty-
first Black trans person murdered so far.
So far, so far, we seem to come, celebrating *National*

Coming Out Day that claimed Sara in Indianapolis.
Two weeks later, Angel in Memphis. Everyday
I checked for news, hung in hope for an end

of violence, of death. Every day I held my breath
until I knew who'd been slain by stranger or lover
as autumn uncovered the bony limbs of trees.

November 4, Skylar Heath mourned as *he;*
on the seventeenth, Yunieski in Miami. *Day
of Trans Remembrance*, November twentieth,

Chae'Meshia chased down by a man with a gun,
and Asia, who said she was going on a date.
Even chronicling this—the daily plunge to heartache—

exhausts me. I wish I didn't have this need to record
what came before what follows here. One by one,
each name, each life: Kimberly the oldest at fifty-five,

Jaheim for her pantsuit, Courtney on Christmas,
and Alexandria, the last of the year, Boxing Day.
Year ends and year begins. On Epiphany, Tyanna,

then Samuel, Bianca, Dominique, Fifty Bandz,
Alexus, Chyna, JJ and Jasmine, Jenna, Diamond,
Rayanna, Jaida, Dominique, Remy, Tiara, Natalia,

Iris, Tiffany, Keri, Jahaira, Whispering Wind,
Sophie, Danika, Serenity, Ollie—only seventeen—
Thomas, Poe, EJ, Aidelen, Taya, Shai, Tierramarie,

Miss CoCo, and Pooh. Names taken to reflect new lives.
It's September 4, 2021. That's the count to August 23.
Thirty-five trans lives taken in eight months. Thirty-five,

the average life expectancy; mid-life, all the sweetness
denied: to grow wise, get fat, find love, make home.
I need to name this, the brutality of tallying the dead.

Horror in equal measure, that they can and must
be counted. Over halfway through a new year, new era,
some might say, the list of names rolls out, rolls on.

I'm here, not just counting, but incanting.

Marilyn Cazares, 22, Brawley, CA, July 16

She was strong and she would look anybody in the eye and say, 'I'm very proud of who I am.'

Marilyn, it's hard to keep up with the pace of hate
this year. This summer, it seems to flower
like a noxious weed, sending spores to couch
themselves into what should be the beauty
of your freedom to be yourself, brave,
your proud Aunt Lorissa's proud niece.

It's rare for family to use the word *niece*
for those who are transgender, as if they hate
recognizing their changed, their brave
children. Is it so hard to let them flower,
to allow them to find their own beauty?
All that imposed invisibility is couched

in misgendering and deadnaming. Your couch
was set ablaze, Marilyn, Aunt Lorissa's niece,
by someone who had to kill your beauty
to cover over his own self-hate.
Did he see in you the seed and flower
of a life he did not feel the bravery

to love? To love what is, we must brave
life or risk watching it go by from the couch,
separated by walls and doors from the flowering.
We must be willing to witness living. My own niece
has also been hurt at the hands of one who hates
her self-sufficiency, her fierce beauty.

Our family nickname for her is *beauty heart.*
It's a way of saying, let my love make you brave,
protect you from the world's random acts of hate.
Marilyn, I'm telling you this only as a way to couch
the heartache of your Aunt proclaiming you as niece.
She told the world about your painful flowering

from a boyhood of taunts and hurt. You were a flower
amidst the heavy feet of those who fear unfamiliar beauty,
one born a boy who grows up to be a niece.
That transition is the thing that made you, Marilyn, brave.
Your murder and the burning of your body on a couch
did not extinguish your beauty with the flames of hate.

Your people came to leave flowers for your bravery,
Marilyn. Your beauty lives beyond the burnt couch.
No one can kill your Aunt Lorissa's niece with hate.

Dior T. Ova/Tiffany Harris, 32, Bronx, NY, July 26

Dior, today my friends asked me what it means
to be Queer. I said it means not being limited
by orientation or gender.
                    Your mother said
he was just gay and that sometimes you liked
to dress up in women's clothes and be feminine.
He didn't hurt anyone.

In 2014, your Facebook profile calls you *him*.
Your photos are cute, Queer, femme.

I read that you went to prison for five years in 2016
for armed robbery, which explains the absence of photos.

When you came out, you were changed.

Your stepfather said you were stabbed twice in the neck,
once in the chest, and once in the abdomen.
How can anyone be so brutal?

Some of your friends didn't know you were back
on early release.
                    Some knew you as Tiffany Harris,
some as Dior H. Ova. They all knew you were *the life
of the party, a shop-a-holic.* Everyone loved you.

Your boyfriend stabbed you in the hallway of your Bronx
apartment at 1:30 on Sunday morning. He was captured
on video wearing a mask to protect himself from COVID.
But his face is clear. I can't tell what he's thinking.
Whether he's coming or leaving.

Dior, Tiffany: your names show your love
of beauty, precious things, elegant, and well-made.

Queasha D. Hardy, 24, Baton Rouge, LA, July 27

I love the skin I'm in and theres nothing you can say or do that's gonna stop gods plan.

Though she lived as a woman, police identified her
as ▮▮▮▮ Hardy, saying Hardy's next of kin requested
she be identified as male. Baton Rouge police do not believe
Hardy was targeted because she was a trans woman.

So she was misgendered, as ▮▮▮▮ Hardy's next of kin requested,
not recognizing the one known as Queasha, who lived as a woman.
Hardy wasn't targeted because she was a trans woman; police say
they've got no other motive for her shooting.

Her killer must've recognized her as Queasha, who lived as a woman—
surely the way she was dressed, her hair and makeup—
what possible motive could there be to explain her shooting
on a rainy day, in the street, in the middle of the afternoon.

Surely she was being herself, had done her hair and makeup,
was on her way somewhere, possibly to the salon to work,
a rainy day, in the street, in the middle of the afternoon,
when someone shot her and left her there alone to die.

Queasha was on her way; ran her own salon, proud of her work
although on a Monday afternoon in July, she must've been free
when someone shot her and left her there alone to die.
We still don't know where she was going or why she died.

On that last Monday afternoon in July, she was still free
to dream her dreams, to simply be herself, Queasha,
wherever it was she was going before she died,
loving the skin she was in, still following God's plan.

Aja Raquelle Rhone-Spears, 34, Portland, OR, July 28

Few details are known about her death, which occurred at a vigil for another homicide victim.

Rocky, if I may call you that, your sense of fashion
is apparent in every photo. It's clear that you were vigilant
about your looks: clothes, makeup, hair, nothing to murder
you for. A month has passed, and still the Portland police
hold no one accountable. There's no more protest
for you, despite being killed by an anonymous brutality.

It's been a hard summer. So many ways to be brutal
erupting like flash fires. I sit here trying to fashion
a response, to find the words that will stand in protest
for your death, a Black trans woman killed at a vigil
for a Black man shot, nothing do to with the police
who, we could say, started this with George Floyd's murder.

We must not forget his and all the other murders,
countless, unending, that show our basic human brutality.
I know it's pointless to lay the blame on the police
who are doing the job that White folks have fashioned
for them. So we do our best now to watch, be vigilant
about what's done in our names. I write these poems of protest,

living far from the streets, the epicenters where protest
looks like a wall of living bodies. Still, there are murders
like Summer Taylor's at the Black Femme March, also a vigil.
An angry man drove his car into dancing bodies. His brutality
not even called murder after killing a young person in that fashion
and badly injuring another. How can we trust the police?

I was taught long ago that they were our friends, the police,
the people you would go to for help. During violent racial protest
in my town, those cops gave my father permission, in a fashion,
to kill whoever got too close. Just drag him inside, not murder.
I remember how the fires burned and gun shots brutalized
a Sunday night, how, in our fear, my family gathered to keep vigil.

Your hometown, another Black man shot, you, Rocky, kept vigil
on the street, then inside someone's home. Later, the police
called about a disturbance, they found you stabbed brutally,
silent witnesses *hostile and uncooperative,* a kind of protest.
They're still not talking about how or why you were murdered.
Whether accident or intention, someone killed you in either fashion.

Kee Sam, 24, Lafayette, LA, August 13, 2020

Kee. Shaki. Queasha. Draya. Black trans women murdered
in Louisiana, which has no law for hate crimes against gender.

Shot on August 13, why was her death lost to us?
Why misfiled under her deadname, ██████, misgendered?

Kee, shot in a hotel and left to die by a sixteen-year-old boy.
What did he know of who she was? Does he know *his* gender?

Four killed by gun violence in Louisiana in four months.
Isn't it time for a trans hate crime law to be engendered?

Subhaga mourns them all through poetry, her people, her sisters;
she carries their deaths in her heart, Queer, Queer-gendered.

Lea Rayshon Daye, 28, Cleveland, OH, August 30

Lea Rayshon Daye, 28, passed away on Aug. 30 after spending more than 100 days in the Cuyahoga County Jail.

There's a time for euphemism and a time for truth.
In a letter to her mother, Lea described the hell
of the last 100 days of her life.

To say she *passed away* in Cuyahoga County Jail—
when in fact she was tormented, raped by inmates and guards,
slept on cell floors, with only gruel to eat—

only adds to the cruelty. The letter was never mailed
but found in her cell among her personal things;
such a letter would never have made it out.

The men in black is what she called the guards
who repeatedly raped her so knew her *intimately.*
Her death is *an extension of lynching* it's been said.

Half of Black trans women spend time in jail,
thirty percent at some time homeless. Where's
the justice in such a life?

Elie Che, 23, Bronx, NY, August 31: An Erasure from Her GoFundMe Page

vulnerable   black trans femme   survival

transitioning

trans life

black trans women   average life span   35

years   I want to make it past that.

I'm not the most passable

don't have a job

NYC   the   place for me to   thrive

through my   changes

a community   queer people

of color.

major mood swings   isn't good to

be around my family   a sensitive time for me   for them   as

they   adjust   to my life   I'm   on my own

your help   I desperately need.

I've got

dysphoria and body dysmorphia   hair on my body

don't want   anymore

also   my adam's apple.

I'm constantly evolving

to love the body   I've been

placed in,   marks and scars   I am

learning to embrace   serving fantasies

with fashion looks,   it's just me hiding behind   my reality.

I want   a different reality

Please please   my survival is from

these donations   and   love.

Isabella Mia Lofton, Brooklyn, NY, September 7, 2020: A Belle Absente

From a Brooklyn rooftop
Labor Day mostly over,
maybe alcohol, maybe sex,
maybe pushed, maybe fell
to the pavement and broke her neck.

What do we know about her
but Chicago, New York,
video dancing in wig and lace,
long nailed, plump lipped,
curvy, feminine, alive?

We know this: One more died
too soon. Someone wrote:
it's no crime if you trick him,
I notice the possible trickery
of words and their cruelty.

Another trans woman lost
to what's unknown. I look
for things to hold as truth:
words, actions, faults found
to close this story with.

Sorrow has its own story.
Birth, childhood, youth
that burns for taboo, for wild
nights, hook ups, and fright
from night's razor-sharp brink.

No one's said her age. Young,
under thirty-five, the most
a trans woman such as she
can expect to be among
the breathing, not a ghost.

Months pass in this year of chaos;
so much taken by force, thirty
murdered, more wounded
in body and twin-spirit: burned,
cut, shot, drowned, dosed.

I write this for her, for them, to lift
their lives from the snippet of news
showing *no proof of crime.* To protect
their freedom to be unmolested, to live.
Someone must honor their chosen selves.

Crossings

Everyone was someone else.
I was a stranger, stray guest. Weed
and coke, shots and beer. Laughter
and heavy bass that thumped like a pulse.

Ignorant, silent, stoned. Legs bare
under suede miniskirt, and vest
over naked chest, leather strap
around my brow, braids, and Halloween
war paint on my cheeks,
                              I lay and let
a woman stroke my skin, shoulder to wrist.
Her lifted skirt revealed the hidden heft
neatly tucked in pantyhose. The scales
of desire shifted. A wink, an eyebrow twitch,
she slapped my calf, adjusted herself, and left.
Decades later, there's regret.

Mia Green, 29, Philadelphia, PA, September 28

The more visible we are, the more we can talk about how bad things are, hopefully it will humanize us and people will see us just like everybody else.

The driver told police his passenger had been shot.
He was racing to a hospital. That was why he ran
a stop sign in his Jeep. She was bleeding from the neck,
where he'd shot her—three times—with a gun lodged in the console
after an argument. He was not a stranger, but her intimate partner
of long standing. His story, it goes without saying, was a lie.

Why is it that so many men feel compelled to lie
about their transgender lovers, the desire that shoots
through them in spite of themselves. Desire can be partner
to violence. Some people need that extra thrill that runs
their breath ragged. Some taboo they've set up that consoles
themselves for what they want like a noose around the neck.

This man, her lover, shot Mia in the arm, side, and neck
with a gun that was at hand while he drove. What was it that lie
between them, that Monday morning? What consolation
in shooting her? She sat by his side in his car, and he shot
her. Now she's dead, and her time and her love of life have run
out. What is love when it turns to killing if not a partner

to hate? Where's the safety in a loaded gun, that gun your partner,
a part of yourself, it's there by your side, a noose around your neck?
Thankfully, we no longer hang killers. How to understand why he ran
so fast to try to save her when he himself had shot her? He tried to lie,
poorly thought through, no story to explain how she'd been shot.
Did he grieve for her death? Was he sorry? Who will be there to console

him? No. He's going to be on his own now, no Mia, no consolation
for his anger or his grief. The paradox of love and hate in partner
crimes is a mystery with deep roots. Every year, countless women are shot
by those who call them mates. Such love is a millstone around their necks.
For trans women, their choices can be dangerous, often resulting in a lie
about who and what they are for fear that love and comfort will run.

Mia and Abdullah Ibn El-Amin Jaamia had their long-term run.
He was no stranger to her or who she was. It does nothing to console
those left behind and grieving, the fear that they will die if they don't lie
about themselves, or hide behind closed doors. They deserve to partner,
to live in truth, love, safety at home. Why must they risk their necks
to have what we all want, to be who and how we are without being shot.
This year is nearly run out. Still, trans women are killed by partners
and, though it's no consolation, strangers. It's a killing bottleneck:
lack of laws, and lies about sex. How long until another lover is shot?

Michelle "Michellyn" Ramos Vargas, 33, San Germán, Puerto Rico, September 30

She had been shot several times in the head. Police are investigating whether her killing may have been a hate crime, but they are not ruling out any possibility.

The prosecutor said that there were three bullet casings
at the scene of the crime, an isolated roadside, near a farm,
that corresponded to three wounds to the face.

She was studying nursing. She was a bartender.
She was calm and reserved and talked to her mother,
who mourns the crime of those three bullet casings.

Her hair was honey-colored, shoulder-length, and curled
away from her face. Her hair was dark brown and pulled back
in pictures before those three wounds to her face.

There were three casings, three wounds. Her face
in photographs is both beautiful and serene. Undamaged.
The prosecutor said that there were three bullet casings.

They are violating us, hunting us, they are murdering us
while Wanda Vázquez and her government chooses to look away
from the three fatal wounds to Michellyn's face.

She was two years short of the average trans life span.
She was the sixth to die in Puerto Rico, the thirtieth in the US.
The prosecutor said that there were three bullet casings
that corresponded to three wounds to the face.

Felycya Harris, 33, Augusta, GA, October 3

Though Georgia passed landmark hate crime legislation this year . . . gender identity is not included.

She was shot
one time.
She was the third
transgender person
killed
in the area
in the last year.

She was left
dying in a park
on a Saturday
in October.
           She was
an interior designer,
a dancer, a friend.

She was the thirty-
first transgender
person killed
this year.

Brook, 32nd in October

Today, the 32nd death appeared,
       found her way to the slow news
              of such things. Another murder

in a land of murders. Another Black
       trans woman killed, the few words,
              small item, scant details. They come

in clusters, *strange fruit.* Sweet
       and tart, their faces made up, hair done,
              sexy poses and clothes, high femme.

Shot and left to die, stabbed, hung,
       bodies burned in cars, on a couch.
              Thirty-two like the gun.

I carry the weight of them. The shards
       of their broken lives in my heart
              like bullets, like knives, like fire.

Brooklyn DeShauna Smith, 20, Shreveport, LA, October 7: An Erasure

It has happened again.

gun shot   20-year-old Black trans woman
       born and raised in Shreveport   studied cosmetology
       worked   a call center   was full
of positivity, good humor,   family support –   typical
     young woman   vibrant   eager to embrace   the world

     turned 20 on September 20, 2020   celebrated with loved ones. Then
– shot and left to die

           the 32nd trans   gender nonconforming
  murder   to date in 2020 in the United States   21st Black trans person
   20th Black trans woman   5th person from Louisiana, all
    Black trans women.   one of 12   age 25 or younger   one of
the four youngest   Yampi   19, Helle   20,
and Brayla   17.

Sara Blackwood, 29, Indianapolis, IN, October 11: National Coming Out Day

Friend, have you walked the streets of your city
under its familiar night sky, safe in your skin,
your body moving inside the clothes you wore
all day, late, work ended. Safe in the familiar
landscape?
        Sara Blackwood might have felt that
on the half hour walk home from her shift
past the White Castle, Popeye's, Catalina Sports
Bar; past the library, the Good News Ministries,
to where E. Washington becomes residential,
safe within herself, thinking of anime, or Avery
waiting for her.
        But then there was a man with a gun
who pulled her into some bushes in the front yard
of a home. The surveillance video shows a flash,
the shot that killed her, Sara's last light.

Sara, *a shy trans woman* bothering no one, her job
at Kroger's, waiting tables at Long John Silver.
Her love for *My Little Pony*. A life so benign,
who would shatter it? Shoot her in the dark and leave
her, yes, her too, to die alone on the street.

Sara, I'm grieving for you, for all of us, who trust
the night, who walk in the dark, cautious, who never
really think of murder, of the brief terror, the loud bullet,
the power in those who don't know or care who we are.

Angel Haynes, 25, Memphis, TN, October 25

They really don't like people like that over there.

There being Whitehaven, informally known
as *Blackhaven*, a conservative neighborhood
south of Memphis. They really don't like
people like that in too many places this year.

People, people, what have we come to?
Whatever happened to *live and let live*?
Whatever happened to *all God's children*?

Angel Unique, she was called, who transitioned
right after high school, in 2013. On the last Sunday
night in October, still healing from surgery to confirm
her gender, with her new breasts, she stopped at a Motel 6
on her way to Memphis where someone shot her in the head
sometime after 2 am.

           Everybody that knew Angel
knew that she was very funny. Very nice to everybody
she met.

Skylar Heath, 20, Miami, Fl, November 4

Once again, a big delay in the news.

Skylar Heath, shot, believed murdered,
on November 4. A month later, we don't
know who killed her or why. Deadnamed
and misgendered, even in her obituary.

The picture is of Skylar with her hair long and sleek,
and smoothed on her brow, those fine baby hairs.
Yet her life history:
>   born to Yolanda,
>   adopted by the late Arlean,
>   raised by a late grandmother
>   and great-grandmother,
>   schools attended and graduated from,
the pronouns are all wrong. ██████████ *Heath.*

A kind and gentle soul, loved family, people
in general . . . nothing short of amazing, he
left us too soon. Friends, he left some time
ago, ██████, to live as Skylar and die as her.

Yunieski Carey Herrera, 39, Miami, FL, November 17

The freeze has returned. Sunrise flares
over the near hills turning the view
pink and blue, the colors of the trans flag.

Another trans woman has been killed. Winter
approaching even in Miami, where her man,
who got her name tattooed on his hip,

jealous and tweaked out on meth, stabbed
her with a knife and fork at 4:00 in the morning
a time we should all be sleeping, for a short

while safe in our own bodies and dreams. Snow
turns blood red as day comes on here far north
of her death. A beauty Queen, salsa dancer,

she told him she'd found *a better man*.
Through his tears he told them this.
In the picture, he's built like an exclamation

point, all upper body bulk, like a wedge
against her sibilant curves. A knife and fork,
tools to devour what sustains us.

Asia Jynaé Foster, 22, Houston, TX, November 20, Transgender Day of Remembrance

She said she was going on a date.

I should be used to the lack of news, but for Asia,
only one article about her death even ten days out.
The thirty-ninth murder of a transgender person
this year, the twenty-third Black, the third
in Texas, and the first in Houston.
       With this silence
about their deaths, it's almost impossible to keep track.
Three days after Asia, the fortieth trans murder,
twenty-fourth Black trans person, was killed in Virginia.

It's not normal for her to leave not in her own car
so it must have been someone she already knew
and had been talking to.

Chae'Meshia Simms, 30, Richmond, VA, November 20, Transgender Day of Remembrance, Again

Feel her fear. Running at night from a man
with a gun, running onto a stranger's porch
and calling out a random name hoping someone
would come.
                But no. The video shows that he caught her
and robbed her. Then there's a gap.

She was found 5 miles away, shot once,
in her mom's rental car, the sole occupant,
crashed into a garage.

Her family says she was driving home.

In the video, he's wearing a dark Nike hoodie
and a surgical mask over a visible goatee.
They've got him described down to cut up, stone-
washed jeans, and brown Timberland boots.
But they do not have him in the flesh.

Her father said *she was well loved, always*
caring for others. We're never going to stop
looking. We're never going to stop looking.

I Have Room for You in Me: A Litany

For the handsome trans woman and cisgender wife,
for the suit and tie and heels, for the skirt and corset
and beard, I have room. No one can say a life is not right.
I have room for you in me. For the one whose father

loved her like a *son* until she became one, I have room
for you in me. For those who claim their own names,
break free from the limited *born-as* cocoon, for the one
with the wide-hipped sashay, big hands smoothing her dress,

I have room for you in me.

For him whose voice rings high, whose chest bears scars
under hair and ink, I have room. For the one who wears
their self-made clothes and hand-painted shoes, not trying to pass,
I have room for you in me. For the pregnant man, and woman father,

I have room for you in me. For the sex worker's food
and rent. For the elderly boy's sparse whiskers and soft eyes.
For the statuesque matron, the broad beamed man; for your lives
and your loves and your rights, I have room.

I have room for you in me.

Kimberly Fial, 55, San Jose, CA, November 22

A butcher knife.   A knife and fork.   A cutting tool.
          Burned on a couch,   in a car.   Shot for having sex
with a man who did   or did not know   she was trans.

          Shot by a teenager,   a long-time partner.   Strangled.
Killed while on vacation,   while at work,   on New Year's
          Day,   the 4th of July,   on Christmas,   just before or after
her birthday.

          Kimberly Susan Fial was not killed
because she was trans.   She was one of five stabbed
          with a butcher knife   while volunteering at the home
that sheltered her when she needed it.

                    Working
alongside another longtime resident   and volunteer
          at Grace Baptist Church,   putting out mats that night
for people to sleep on.

          She was killed because the world
is unsafe,   some people are sick,   violence is endemic,
          systems fail.

          Trans people are anywhere
                              between eleven and forty percent
          of the homeless population.

                    It's a window
you could drive a truck through.

          Her friends said   *She did everything right.*

               We.   Still.   Failed.   Her.

Jaheim Bella Pugh, 19, Prichard, AL, December 18

He said, 'I just wanna be me momma. I just wanna be me,' is what he said and I support him.

It seems to come down to the rainbow jumpsuit
she—dressed as a woman, Jaheim was Bella was she—
wore to a Christmas party. That and the wig.

Bystanders videotaping her while she lay dead
or dying in the street said *He would still be alive*
if he wasn't wearing that dress. Not even a dress,
just a woman's colorful, one-piece pantsuit.

Courtney Eshay Key, 25, Chicago, IL, December 25

She wanted to be something . . . She wanted to beat the odds.

So it seems it will end the way it began, New Year's Day
to Christmas, and still, it wasn't over. Eshay was buried
on the second day. Found Christmas night at 8:35 on the street,
thought to be a hit and run but for the gunshot wounds to her head.
Police and news referred to her as *him*, held her body as *John Doe*.
I wasn't there, but in every picture, Eshay is clearly female-
identified. She was a decade short of those odds—the trans life
expectancy of 35—*was trying to better herself in particular ways.*

The year ends the way it began: in shame.

Alexandria Winchester, 24, Bronx, NY, December 26: An Erasure

she may have known her killer.

was murdered on the streets

because of her identity.

We are shattered   *not broken.*
                    we mourn this loss,   *fight for trans lives,*

say her name,   *trans lives are*
beautiful.

                    The loss
          is devastating.

at least the 44th trans or gender non-conforming person to be murdered in the US in 2020

the worst year since

This/Sister

I fold my jewel-tone panties,
file away my bras by cup type—
each with its own small drawer.
I bend and drop stacks of socks
and feel my woman's body move.

>   These breasts. The soft belly
>   over the part of me that opens
>   inside, layers of labia, flesh
>   of pudenda, all alive.

White, *this-gender*, Queer, in this body
sixty-five years. I do not take for granted
those extra thirty years. My clothes run
from boy to matron. I have the privilege
to wear them, to live only dependent on how I feel.

>   A little butch.
>   A little femme.

My trans brothers and sisters,
no one should have to die for this.

Notes on the Origin and Sources of the Poems

In early July of 2020, I was invited to participate in a workshop to write formal poems of social protest. The first assignment was to find a topic of injustice that spoke to us and then to write either an acrostic for the word Justice, or an Abcedarian. As a Queer person who has been tracking and mourning lost Black trans lives, I started there. Researching the murders of transgender people, I found the Human Rights Campaign page that lists the names and brief bios of transgender and gender nonconforming people who died from violence. The result was the opening poem: "An Acrostic for Justice."

Completing the poem left a hole in me. I wanted to honor and elegize the people named in the acrostic with a poem of their own. From that urge to recognize, these poems were born. All of the information in these poems comes from public records found online: websites, newspapers, and social media. The poems are creations that merge the typically limited information found in these sources with my own imagination and my experience as a Queer person. Most poems include some italicized language spoken or written by the subject or about them by friends, family, and law enforcement personnel. In some instances, I truncated direct quotations for impact. I have blacked out any deadnames quoted in sources. I've done my best to accurately reflect the information about these crimes. Any errors are mine and do not reflect on BOA Editions.

Dustin Parker, 25, McAlester, OK, January 1: "No arrests in murder of McAlester man on New Year's Day." *ABC8 Tulsa.*

Alexa: Neulisa Luciano Ruiz, 28, Toa Baja, Puerto Rico, February 24: *They didn't kill a man in a skirt. They killed Alexa.* Brito, Christopher. "Bad Bunny calls attention to the killing of a transgender woman." *CBS News,* 28 Feb 2020. Her killers' words from their recording of her murder, Riley, John. "Trans Woman Killed In Puerto Rico after Using Women's Bathroom." *MetroWeekly,* 26 Feb 2020. Since her murder, three men were charged with hate crimes: https://www.justice.gov/opa/pr/puerto-rico-men-charged-hate-crimes-shooting-transgender-woman-paintball-gun.

Yampi Mendez Arocho, 19, Moca, Puerto Rico, March 5: *Fuck love; I don't believe in it anymore.* www.facebook.com/yampi.arocho, 4 Mar, 2020.

John Scott/Scottlyn Kelly DeVore, 51, Augusta, GA, March 12: *He still had the same heart no matter what he looked like, which was a good heart, a kind heart.* www.wfxg. com, https://www.facebook.com/scott.devore.90. Two people were indicted in DeVore's murder: https://www.augustachronicle.com/story/news/crime/2021/01/06/augusta-mur-der-indictment-returned-john-scott-devores-death/6565347002/.

Monika Diamond, 34, Charlotte, NC, March 18: Deadnaming and murder details: Kiro7.com

> *I want to give something back*
> *to the mothers in the LGBT community*
> *to say thanks for what you do as a mother*
> *in the LGBT community and this pageant*
> *is for the female in the LGBT community*
> *that is a Drag, FIEF or Transgender.*

International Mother of the Year Pageantry System Facebook Page, https://www.facebook.com/International-Mother-of-the-Year-Pageantry-System-420994091391049.

Lexi, "Ebony" Sutton, 33, Harlem, NY, March 28: *Lexi of the House of Ebony.* Gaycitynews.com.

Johanna Metzger, 25, Baltimore, MD, April 11: I gleaned information from Johanna's Facebook page, https://www.facebook.com/joseph.metzger.334 and from her mother, Christine Marro's, Facebook page. https://www.facebook.com/christine.marro.5.

Serena Angelique Vasquez, 31 & Layla Pelaez Sánchez, 21, Humacao, Puerto Rico, April 21: An Erasure: Extracts from the FBI affidavit reported in the Washington Blade, May 4, 2020.

Penélope Díaz Ramírez, 31, Bayamon, Puerto Rico, April 13: beaten and hanged to death/at the Bayamon correctional complex,/a men's prison in Puerto Rico. Metroweekly.com. A photo was published subsequent to my writing the poem: https://www.hrc.org/news/hrc-mourns-penelope-diaz-ramirez-trans-latina-killed-in-puerto-rico.

Nina Pop, 28, Sikeston, MO, May 3: Most of the quoted material here is taken from her Facebook page: https://www.facebook.com/nina.pop.752 and some from the video posted there taken the night of her death. From Blavity.com "many called to give information."

Helle Jae O'Regan, 20, San Antonio, TX, May 6: "I love myself now. Thank you to everyone who's ever supported me and to anyone who hasn't I hope you come around." HRC.org. Her killer's insistence that *God sent me to kill you for doing something wrong,* lbgtqnation.com.

Jayne Thompson, 33, Mesa County, CO, May 9, 2020: Misgendered for a Month: All quoted material from www.them.us.com.

Tony McDade, 38, Tallahassee, FL, May 27: All quoted material from www.wsfu.com.

Of Band Fags and Hate Mail: *Ask me what difference their greatest love or hate has made,* William Stafford's "Ask Me."

Dominique "Rem'mie" Fells, Philadelphia, PA, June 9: Epigraph and quote from video transcribed from *In Loving Memory, Dominique Rem'mie Fells,* YouTube.com.

> *Rem'mie was just always having a good time*
> *and laughing. We have a lot of family get togethers,*
> *she loved being around her cousins, uncles and aunts.*
> *She likes to eat and have a good time.* Fox29.com

Her mother's and sister's quotes taken from Insider.com. Her killer was sentenced to at least twenty years for the murder: https://www.inquirer.com/news/philadelphia-homi-cides-transgender-women-tameka-washington-dominique-fells-20210726.html.

Riah Milton, 25, Liberty Twp, OH, June 9: *Ohio does not have a hate crime statute that includes sexual orientation or gender identity.* Metroweekly.com. I've included these sorts of statements with some regularity to highlight the both the lack of hate crime laws and the frequent insistence that trans women and men are not targets of hate crimes without any indication of how that's determined. The third suspect was found and charged: https://www.journal-news.com/news/crime--law/cincinnati-man-indicted-multiple-felonies-fa-tal-liberty-twp-shooting/6ynh7IFv07syOABpMJCbNK/.

Selena Reyes-Hernandez, 37, Chicago, IL, May 31: *He kept seeing her face, so he went back there to do it again.* chicago.cbslocal.com.

Brian "Egypt" Powers, 43, Akron, June 13: *He knew so many people . . . He never met a stranger in his life.* Spoken by Egypt's mother, Vivian Powers-Smith. daily-jeff.com.

*As of March 2023, a man has been charged with themurder of Brian "Egypt" Powers: https://www.beaconjournal.com/story/news/crime/2023/03/10/bobby-lee-bell-charged-in-2020-death-of-brian-powers-in-akron/69995618007/.

Brayla Stone, 17, Little Rock, AK, June 25: *You gotta forgive me if u feel I'm too much.* facebook.com/brayla.stone.9. Her killer was convicted and faces 50 years in prison: https://www.metroweekly.com/2021/08/arkansas-man-receives-50-year-prison-sentence-after-pleading-guilty-to-killing-transgender-teen/.

Merci Mack Richey, 22, Dallas, TX, June 30: *I really feel for the victim's family because this now puts them through further grief.* https://www.dallasnews.com/news/crime/2021/11/08/dallas-county-prosecutors-drop-murder-case-against-man-accused-of-killing-transgender-woman/. A previous version of this poem identified the suspect in Mack's murder, but a year later, the case was dismissed due to lack of information. I've revised the poem here to reflect the current state of the case.

Shaki Peters, 32, Amite City, LA, July 1: *She was full of laughter and an abundance of life.* theadvocate.com. This was one of the most difficult poems to write simply because there was so little information about Shaki's death. Most news accounts lumped it in with other murders in Louisiana around the time. There was almost no personal information about her, and that grieved me deeply. Two people were eventually indicted in her death: https://www.livingstonparishnews.com/breaking_news/two-indicted-for-second-degree-murder-for-summer-killing-of-transgender-woman-district-attorney-reports/article_e6831a9c-340e-11eb-9d30-cf40ecfa8f56.html.

Bree Black, 27, Pompano Beach, FL, July 3: *The average life expectancy of a Black trans woman is 35 years of age.* thestranger.com.

Summer Taylor, 24, Seattle, WA, July 4: *They were always the first one to call people out for being sexist, racist — standing up for queer and trans people . . . they were the ones that were so vocal.* nytimes.com. Diaz Love's quotes about death threats is from her Facebook page, https://www.facebook.com/Diaz4LOVE.

Marilyn Cazares, 22, Brawley, CA, July 16: *She was strong and she would look anybody in the eye and say, 'I'm very proud of who I am.'* abc.news.go.com.

Dior H. Ova/Tiffany Harris, 32, Bronx, NY, July 26: lgbtqnation.com/2020/07/police-searching-suspect-stabbing-death-black-transgender-woman/. A suspect has been charged: https://www.norwoodnews.org/kingsbridge-man-wanted-for-questioning-in-connection-to-murder-of-woman/.

Queasha D. Hardy, 24, Baton Rouge, LA, July 27: Lines from stanza one appropriated from aazios.com.

Aja Raquelle Rhone-Spears, 34, Portland, OR, July 28: *Few details are known about her death, which occurred at a vigil for another homicide victim.* people.com.

Lea Rayshon Daye, 28, Cleveland, OH, August 30: *Lea Rayshon Daye, 28, passed away on Aug. 30 after spending more than 100 days in the Cuyahoga County Jail.* cleveland19.com, planettransgender.com.

Isabella Mia Lofton, Brooklyn, NY, September 7, 2020: A Belle Absente, *it's no crime if you trick him.* deleted comment from Twitter.

Aerrion Burnette, 37, Independence, MO, September 19: A Found Poem: https://www.advocate.com/crime/2020/9/25/black-transgender-woman-aerrion-burnett-killed-missouri.

Mia Green, 29, Philadelphia, PA, September 28: *The more visible we are, the more we can talk about how bad things are, hopefully it will humanize us and people will see us just like everybody else:* epgn.com. Her killer has been convicted: https://epgn.com/2022/08/30/killer-of-mia-green-convicted-of-third-degree-murder/

Michelle "Michellyn" Ramos Vargas, 33, San Germán, Puerto Rico, September 30: *She had been shot several times in the head. Police are investigating whether her killing may have been a hate crime, but they are not ruling out any possibility.* medium.com.

Felycya Harris, 33, Augusta, GA, October 3: *Though Georgia passed landmark hate crime legislation this year . . . gender identity is not included.* cbsnews.com. A suspect has been indicted: https://theaugustapress.com/murder-suspect-in-felycya-harris-death-indicted-so-called-gunslinger-unmasked/.

Brooklyn DeShauna Smith, 20, Shreveport, LA, October 7: An Erasure: *It has happened again.* https://www.pghlesbian.com/2020/10/black-trans-woman-brooklyn-deshauna-smith-20-killed-in-shreveport-louisiana/.

Sara Blackwood, 29, Indianapolis, IN, October 11: National Coming Out Day: https://www.metroweekly.com/2020/10/indiana-trans-woman-killed-while-walking-home-on-national-coming-out-day/. Her killer was sentenced to 55 years: https://www.indystar.com/story/news/crime/2020/11/23/sara-blackwood-shooting-johnny-viverette-charged-murder-robbery/6395422002/.

Angel Haynes, 25, Memphis, TN, October 25: *They really don't like people like that over there.* localmemphis.com.

Yunieski Carey Herrera, 39, Miami, FL, November 17: local10.com.

Skylar Heath, 20, Miami, Fl, November 4: advocate.com, paradisemfh.com/obituary/kendrick-heath.

Asia Jynaé Foster, 22, Houston, TX, November 20, Transgender Day of Remembrance: fox26houston.com. A suspect has been charged: https://www.houstontx.gov/police/nr/2022/oct/nr221006-2.htm.

Chae'Meshia Simms, 30, Richmond, VA, November 20, Transgender Day of Remembrance, Again: http://richmondvapolice.blogspot.com, wtvr.com A suspect was arrested in conjunction with her murder: https://www.wtvr.com/news/local-news/man-arrested-in-connection-to-murder-of-richmond-transgender-woman.

Kimberly Fial, 55, November 22, San Jose, CA: https://www.pghlesbian.com/.

Jaheim Bella Pugh, 19, December 18, Prichard, AL: *He said, 'I just wanna be me momma. I just wanna be me,' is what he said and I support him.*pghlesbian.com/. A suspect has been charged: https://abc3340.com/news/local/alabama-man-charged-with-murder-in-shooting-at-christmas-party.

Courtney Eshay Key, 25, December 25, Chicago, IL: An Erasure: chicago.cbslocal.com. A suspect has been arrested: https://chicago.suntimes.com/crime/2022/10/21/23416988/truss-charged-murder-key-chicago-violence.

Alexandria Winchester, 24, December 26, Bronx, NY: An Erasure: out.com/crime/2021/1/07/alexandria-winchester-trans-woman-shot-makes-44-2020-killings. A suspect has been charged in her killing: https://www.metroweekly.com/2021/02/man-indicted-for-fatally-shooting-transgender-woman-in-the-bronx/.

Acknowledgments

My sincerest thanks to the editors of the following publications for printing sometimes earlier versions of many of these poems and helping to share the lives of those lost to violence.

The Bangalore Review: "Penélope Díaz Ramírez, 31, Bayamon, Puerto Rico, April 13," March 2021;

The Bombay Review: "Brayla Stone, 17, Little Rock, June 25," "Merci Mack, Richey, 22, Dallas, June 30;" "Shaki Peters, 32, Amite City, July 1," October 2020;

The Indianapolis Review: "Sara Blackwood, 29, Indianapolis, IN, October 11: National Coming Out Day," April 2021;

The Lavender Review: "Transitory: An Acrostic for Justice," December 2020;

Queerlings: "This/Sister;"

Queer Southeast Asia: A Literary Journal of Transgressive Art: "Cautiously Watching for Violence;" "Selena Reyes-Herandez, 37, Chicago, IL, May 31: A Pantoum;" "Bree Black, 27, Pompano Beach, FL, July 3;" "I Have Room for You in Me: A Litany," January 2022;

Queer Toronto Literary Magazine: "Yampi Mendez Arocho, 19, Moca, Puerto Rico, March 5;" "Monika Diamond, 34, Charlotte, NC, March 18;" "Johanna Metzger, 25, Baltimore, MD, April 11;" "Serena Angelique Vasquez, 31 & Layla Pelaez Sánchez, 21, Humacao, Puerto Rico, April 21: An Erasure;" "Felycya Harris, 33, Augusta, GA, October 3;" "Courtney Eshay Key, 25, Chicago, IL, December 25," November 2021;

Rise Up Review: "Elie Che, 23, Bronx, NY, August 31: Accidental Drowning," February 2020; "Yunieski Carey Herrera, 39, Miami, FL, November 17;" January 2022, "Why I'm Writing about the Murders of Trans & Gender Nonconforming People in the Year of COVID," July 2022;

River Heron Review: "Summer Taylor, 24, Seattle, July 4," September 2020;

Sad Girls Lit Club: "Alexa: Neulisa Luciano Ruiz, 28, Tao Baja, Puerto Rico, February 24," November 2020;

Sea to Sky Review: "Tony McDade, 38, Tallahassee, FL, May 27;" "Aja Raquelle Rhone Spears, 34, Portland, OR, July 28;" "Queasha D. Hardy, 24, Baton Rouge, LA, July 27: A Pantoum;" "Isabella Mia Lofton, Brooklyn, NY, September 7, 2020: A Belle Absente;" "Brooklyn DeShauna Smith, 20, Shreveport, LA, October 7: A Found Poem," November 2021;

Wordpeace: "Nina Pop, 28, Sikeston, MO, May 3;" "Helle Jae O'Regan, 20, San Antonio, TX, May 6;" "Jayne Thompson, 33, Mesa County, CO, May 9, 2020: Misgendered for a Month;" "Dominique "Rem'mie" Fells, Philadelphia, PA, June 8;" "Riah Milton, 25, Liberty Twp, OH, June 9," "Michelle "Michellyn" Ramos Vargas, 33, San Germán, Puerto Rico, September 30."

To my writing groups, the spectacular *Pretzels*, Jennifer Martelli, Brandel France de Bravo, and Barbara O'Dair for their endless readings of original poems and the manuscript as a whole as well as their encouragement to keep sending it out, my endless devotion. To my local Confluence Poets group, thanks for your thoughtful reading and support. Cindy, thank you for those early poems and forms. And to Sugandhi, who also lived through the difficult period of deep sorrow of researching, loving, and speaking for each of the subjects of these poems, and for the perfect cover art, thank you; I love you. To Peter, Gena, Michelle and everyone at BOA, my gratitude is endless. For early reading and commentary, Diane Seuss thank you for modeling what a poem can be, Jill McDonough for *Habeas Corpus* and all your other work, and my dear longtime friend, CA Conrad for still being in my constellation. To the Human Rights Campaign Fund and the National Center for Transgender Equity, thank you for being there.

About the Author

Subhaga Crystal Bacon is the author of four collections of poetry including *Transitory*, recipient of the Isabella Gardner Award for Poetry; *Surrender of Water in Hidden Places*, winner of the Red Flag Poetry Chapbook Prize; *Blue Hunger*, Methow Press, 2020, and *Elegy with a Glass of Whiskey*, BOA Editions, 2004, which won the A. Poulin, Jr. Poetry Prize. Her work has appeared in a variety of print and online publications, and she is a teaching artist in the schools for Methow Arts Alliance and also teaches individual and small groups of adults. A Queer elder, she lives in rural northcentral Washington on unceded Methow land with her partner, the painter, Sugandhi Katharine Barnes, and their Labradoodle, Lola.

BOA Editions, Ltd. American Poets Continuum Series

No. 1 *The Fuhrer Bunker: A Cycle of Poems in Progress*
W. D. Snodgrass

No. 2 *She*
M. L. Rosenthal

No. 3 *Living With Distance*
Ralph J. Mills, Jr.

No. 4 *Not Just Any Death*
Michael Waters

No. 5 *That Was Then: New and Selected Poems*
Isabella Gardner

No. 6 *Things That Happen Where There Aren't Any People*
William Stafford

No. 7 *The Bridge of Change: Poems 1974–1980*
John Logan

No. 8 *Signatures*
Joseph Stroud

No. 9 *People Live Here: Selected Poems 1949–1983*
Louis Simpson

No. 10 *Yin*
Carolyn Kizer

No. 11 *Duhamel: Ideas of Order in Little Canada*
Bill Tremblay

No. 12 *Seeing It Was So*
Anthony Piccione

No. 13 *Hyam Plutzik: The Collected Poems*

No. 14 *Good Woman: Poems and a Memoir 1969–1980*
Lucille Clifton

No. 15 *Next: New Poems*
Lucille Clifton

No. 16 *Roxa: Voices of the Culver Family*
William B. Patrick

No. 17 *John Logan: The Collected Poems*

No. 18 *Isabella Gardner: The Collected Poems*

No. 19 *The Sunken Lightship*
Peter Makuck

No. 20 *The City in Which I Love You*
Li-Young Lee

No. 21 *Quilting: Poems 1987–1990*
Lucille Clifton

No. 22 *John Logan: The Collected Fiction*

No. 23 *Shenandoah and Other Verse Plays*
Delmore Schwartz

No. 24 *Nobody Lives on Arthur Godfrey Boulevard*
Gerald Costanzo

No. 25 *The Book of Names: New and Selected Poems*
Barton Sutter

No. 26 *Each in His Season*
W. D. Snodgrass

No. 27 *Wordworks: Poems Selected and New*
Richard Kostelanetz

No. 28 *What We Carry*
Dorianne Laux

No. 29 *Red Suitcase*
Naomi Shihab Nye

Colophon

BOA Editions, Ltd., a not-for-profit publisher of poetry
and other literary works, fosters readership and appreciation
of contemporary literature. By identifying, cultivating, and publishing both new
and established poets and selecting authors of unique literary talent, BOA brings
high-quality literature to the public.

Support for this effort comes from the sale of its publications, grant funding, and
private donations.

⧗

*The publication of this book is made possible, in part,
by the special support of the following individuals:*

Anonymous x2

Angela Bonazinga & Catherine Lewis

Christopher C. Dahl

Robert & Rae Gilson

James Long Hale

Margaret B. Heminway

Nora A. Jones

Paul LaFerriere & Dorrie Parini, *in honor of Bill Waddell*

Barbara Lovenheim

Richard Margolis & Sherry Phillips

Joe McElveney

Daniel M. Meyers, *in honor of J. Shepard Skiff*

The Mountain Family, *in support of poets & poetry*

Nocon & Associates

Boo Poulin

John H. Schultz

Robert Tortorella

William Waddell & Linda Rubel

Bruce & Jean Weigl